The Color of Love in a Black and White World

Anthony Todd Arnold & Daisy Alex Lloyd

Archway Publishing books may be ordered through booksellers or by contacting:

Archway Publishing
1663 Liberty Drive
Bloomington, IN 47403
www.archwaypublishing.com
1 (888) 242-5904

ISBN: 978-1-4808-8347-5 (sc)
ISBN: 978-1-4808-8346-8 (e)

Library of Congress Control Number: 2019915353

Print information available on the last page.

Archway Publishing rev. date: 10/10/2019

"Wisdom is the principal thing: therefore get wisdom; and with all thy getting get understanding" (PROVERBS 4:7 KJV).

CONTENTS

PREFACE

When I ask people for an answer to this simple question, "Why do you think people can only see other people in the color of black or white?" The consistent meaningless answer given most often is this, "You know that's really a good question." Honestly, far too many people simply concede that question is far too complicated for them to answer. So, people find themselves bogged down in endless philosophical debates, useless theological arguments, and pondering meaningless religious metaphors seeking to find an acceptable answer. Universally, most people think "if they cannot see it; then it's probably not real." In other words, people only believe what they can see intuitively. On the other hand, everything known is not based on what people can taste, touch, smell, feel, or observe. Clearly, all rational- minded people agree that you can feel the air but you cannot see the air.

Suffice to say, fleshly cut flowers are dead the moment they are severed from the stem. Albeit, flowers cut from the stem may retain their color for a few days nonetheless they are still dead. Likewise, people who sever themselves from God are as flowers cut from the stem. Concurrently, people may live for many years, nonetheless, they are still considered dead. "I am the true vine, and my Father is the gardener. He cuts off every branch of mine that does not produce fruit. He also trims every branch that produces fruit to prepare it to produce even more. You have already been prepared to produce more fruit by the teaching I have given you. Stay joined to me and I will stay joined to you. No branch can produce fruit alone. It must stay connected to the vine. It is the same with you. You cannot produce fruit alone. You must stay joined to me" (JOHN 15:1-4 ERV).

INTRODUCTION

The purpose of this book is to provide the reader with an understanding of this multipart question people all over the world, pretend is unknowable, "Where do I come from, and why am I here?" In other words, "Who created me and what is my purpose?" Truthfully, God is the Creator of all living things, and by his virtue, he created people to live in an unbroken relationship with him. Clearly, the endless processional of new life born every day is the immutable proof that God is the source of all life. Therefore, "Who created me, and what is my purpose" is now understood. "For ever since the creation of the world His invisible nature and attributes, that is, His eternal power and divinity, have been made intelligible and clearly discernible in and through the things that have been made (His handiworks)" (ROMANS 1: 20 AMP). Nonetheless, most people still question whether God is the source of all life. For that reason, wicked people persuade naive people all over the world into placing their complete trust in their insane religious beliefs, evil-minded customs, and backward traditions.

Hideously, far too many Muslim children die tragically in Arabic speaking countries believing they are doing "the will of Allah" when called to duty by their religious leaders to carry out the insane act of "Istishhad." *Istishhad* is the

Arabic word for "heroic death." The desire of these wicked people is achieved when children misguidedly agree to detonate an explosive vest aimed to kill as many people as possible as the child's ultimate gift of love. "If you say, "But we didn't know about this," won't he who weighs the heart consider it? Won't he who protects your life know? Won't he repay a person according to his work?" (PROVERBS 24:12 CSB)

CHAPTER 1

Color Blind

In American lexicon when a person says, I am *"color-blind"* that means they see every person equal regardless of *skin color*. Actually, nothing could be further from the truth because the bedrock of American culture is based on racial prejudice. The practice of racial prejudice is well-documented beginning when the first European settlers referred to their Native American host as "Redskins." Albeit, this obscene culture of racial prejudice based merely on *skin color* is not exclusive to American culture. Nonetheless, it is the most recognizable model in modern history. All based on whether a person's *skin color* is black or white. Therefore, the term *color-blind* in American culture meaning *skin color* is insignificant is just untrue.

Historically, *skin color* was first used with evil intent by some fiendish British colonist to destroy the minds of the Native Americans Indians. The aim of the British invaders was to divide, destroy, or conquer every Indian nation using *skin color* as a psychological weapon of warfare. Factually, prior to the seventeenth century, Indians and Europeans rarely mention the color of each other's skin. In fact, *skin color* was only used to differentiate the Native American tribes, but never used in a derogatory manner with evil intent. Nevertheless, using *skin color* to degrade, segregate, or elevate the status of one group of people over another is well documented in the chronicles of history.

Honestly, *skin color* prejudice is still widely taught specifically by misguided Caucasian Americans using fear to accomplish their purpose. *Fear,* "a distressing emotion aroused by impending danger, evil, pain, etc., whether the threat is real or imagined; the feeling or condition of being afraid." In reality, *Fear* is a *"living spirit"* indiscernible by physical sight and opposes the things of God. Its intention is to vilify God, so people completely reject God as the source of human prosperity. Furthermore, the *spirit of fear* understands that people living in a continuous state of fear suffer from extreme anxiety that diminishes people's confidence, and damages their vision. "Where there is no vision [no redemptive revelation of God], the people perish" (PROVERBS 29:18(a) AMP). Consequently, people who have no revelation are not just *color blind*, but completely blind.

Truthfully, the *spirit of fear* has no divine power to possess the minds of people, but it can influence their thinking. Likewise, the *spirit of fear* cannot enter into a person's body; however, it possesses the power to manipulate the way people think. For that reason, devilish-minded people (under the sway of the *spirit of fear*) accomplish their goal by causing people to believe they don't need God. Concurrently, their aim is to trick as many people as possible to see themselves as independent "free will" agents not answerable to God. Finally, their combined objective is achieved when people voluntarily sever their relationship with God. On the other hand, God created all people with the power to overcome the influence of the *spirit of fear*. However, that authority is granted only to those who maintain an unbroken relationship with God. "I call heaven and earth to record this day against you, *that* I have set before you life and death, blessing and cursing: therefore choose life that both thou and thy seed may live" (DEUTERONOMY 30:19 NLT). Make no mistake there are two real spirits; the *Spirit of life* (God); and the *spirit of fear* (death). Therefore, choose God (life) and live, or choose the *spirit of fear*, and die.

With that in mind, William Bruce Jenner born October 28, 1949 (age 70) is an American Olympic gold medalist winning decathlete. Bruce Jenner is considered "heroic" to some people because of his proven ability to improvise, adapt, and rise above many societal norms. In April 2015, Bruce Jenner publicly announced his decision to reassign (change) his gender to female. In September 2016 Bruce Jenner legally changed his name to "Caitlyn Jenner" and changed his gender classification from male to female. Finally, in January 2017 Caitlyn Jenner underwent sex reassignment surgery making her one of the most infamous transgender women in the world. Consequently, the goal of the *spirit of fear* is achieved when people to do the vilest things to themselves and to others. "Pride precedes destruction; an arrogant spirit appears before a fall" (PROVERBS 16:18 ISV).

Surely, Caitlyn Jenner's decision to change her gender surgically is the most appalling example of a person under the sway of the *spirit of fear*. "Therefore God gave them up in the lust of their [own] hearts to sexual impurity, to the dishonoring of their bodies among themselves [abandoning them to the degrading power of sin], because they exchanged the truth of God for a lie and worshiped and served the creature rather than the Creator, Who is blessed forever! Amen (so be it)" (ROMANS 1:24−25 AMP). For that reason, people under the sway of the *spirit of fear* repeatedly do the most inconceivable things to hurt themselves and to hurt others.

Needless to say, any rational thinking person inherently knows, understands, and comprehends no one possesses the "absolute" power to change the nature of anything. Clinically, only the insane feel they need to alter, change, or augment their bodies based on how they "feel" about something, someone, or themselves. Honestly, "Is the clay greater than the Potter?" Can the clay say to the Potter, "What shall you do with me?" Likewise, can the clay take the shape of its choosing? In like manner, can the characters tell the illustrator who they will be? The answer is simply no because "the servant is never greater than his Master."

CHAPTER 2

The Color of Imagination

Have you heard the cliché *"silence is deafening"*? It is a cliché about expecting a response and not getting one. In fact, no one can expect to get a response without first speaking a command. Generally speaking, most people are familiar with this basic principle, although it may not be known specifically to them as the *"call and respond"* principle. The *"call and response"* principle simply means expecting a response when a question or command is given. For example, "Is it raining?" That question reflects the "call" part of that principle. "Yes, it is raining", reflects the "response" part of that principle. Truthfully, no one is capable of accomplishing anything without the authority to command because command means to authorize someone to achieve something.

A *Command* is "to direct with specific authority." Most people believe what they hear is made possible through the workings of the physical ear, i.e. the outer ear, the middle ear, the inner ear, and that is true because God created the physical ear to distinguish sounds. Realistically, the true function of hearing is the ability to perceive a thing, or an event that appears vividly to the mind. Consequently, the real job of hearing is to create a picture that appears vividly in the mind when a command is given. Therefore, hearing is a result of what is commanded not as a result of what people hear through the workings of the physical ear. In other words, God created people to see based on what hear not based on what they see.

For that reason, God established this divine sequence "to command, to see, and to achieve." *Divine* means appropriated from God. *Sequence* means the established series (order), or succession. In fact, before a person can "wake up", sit up or stand up they must hear the command causing them to see the activity vividly in their mind before achieving it.

"Ears to hear and eyes to see— both are gifts from the LORD" (PSALMS 94:9 NLT).

Factually, most people never consider how they achieve anything until a severe injury occurs and their mobility, dexterity, flexibility, or mental capacity is diminished. Frankly, everyone will experience some kind of physical injury between the cradles and the grave. In fact, it is only in those circumstances when people have a "reality check" they are not self-made. Still, most people will not concede they are created by God. Nevertheless, God created everything to prosper in the divine sequence so that every living thing can hear, see, and achieve a task commanded. "So God created man in His own image, in the image and likeness of God He created him; male and female He created them. And, God blessed them and said to them, "Be fruitful, multiply, and fill the earth, and subdue it [using all its vast resources in the service of God and man]; and have dominion over the fish of the sea, the bird's of the air, and over every living creature that moves upon the earth" (GENESIS 1:27, 28 AMP). For that reason, all living creatures are subordinate and under the authority of people.

Clearly, people possess the power to command the largest animal's in the world, i.e. killer whales, elephants, lions, tigers, bears, etc. to perform routine duties under their command. In the same way, people routinely demonstrate their ability to train the smallest of insects, i.e. bees, fleas, and ants to perform a variety of tasks under their command. Furthermore, people possess the authority to dispatch birds to carry messages across oceans, rivers, seas, and remote landmasses to a precise location confident the birds under their command will accomplish their task.

Therefore, it is ludicrous to question any other source of life except the Living God who is the Author and Finisher all life. Suffice to say no one can truthfully say, "I do not know who created me? And I do not know why he created me?"

In addition, God created all living things with the attribute to imagine. *Imagine* is to form a picture that appears vividly in the mind although not actually present. Actually, in order to achieve something, you must be able to imagine something. In fact, what people see is the evidence of what they imagined. In other words, you cannot see what you cannot imagine because what you see is the result of what you imagined. Literally, before a person can achieve any physical task, i.e. sit up, stand up or take one step they must imagine it before they can achieve it. Surely, no one believes a shoe can place itself on a person's foot. Realistically, a person must imagine (see the shoe in their mind) before putting a shoe on their foot. Again, before a person can achieve something they must imagine something.

For example, Orville Wright, born (1871) in Dayton, Ohio, and his younger brother Wilbur Wright are the inventors of the first successful airplane. Factually, these two brothers successfully conducted the first free controlled power-driven airplane on December 17, 1903. Clearly, the airplane is the evidence of what these two pioneers in aviation imagined. In other words, the plane didn't imagine, command, and create the Wright brothers; instead, the plane is the result of what the Wright brothers imagined. Consequently, the first power-driven airplane they build is the irrefutable proof of the attribute to imagine. "Shall the potter be considered of no more account than the clay? Shall the thing that is made say of its maker, He did not make me; or the thing that is formed say of him who formed it, He has no understanding?" (ISAIAH 29:16(b) AMPC). Nonetheless, most people are willing to spend a lifetime on a pointless quest to prove God isn't real.

Finally, God created all living things with the divine attribute to create. *Create* "is to cause something to come into being, as something unique that would not naturally evolve or that is not made by an ordinary process." Truthfully, no rational thinking person would dispute that birds build their own nest from materials gathered in the earth, i.e. twigs, branches, leaves, and other natural materials. Just as no one believes there is a "Bird School of Architectural Design" that teaches birds how to build a nest independent of their Creator. Equally, no one believes that honey bees attend a "Bee Hive School of Design" that teaches bees how to build a beehive independent of their Creator. "The Lord has made everything [to accommodate itself and contribute] to its own end *and* His own purpose–even the wicked [are fitted for their role] for the day of calamity *and* evil" (PROVERBS 16:4 AMP).

CHAPTER 3

The Color of Love

What is the first color that comes into your mind when you think about love? Is it the color red symbolizing endless love? Is it the color of white symbolizing the purity of love? Is it the color of honey symbolizing the intimacy of love? Whatever color that comes into your mind really doesn't matter because people use every color to express their love for someone or something except *skin color*. In fact, people from every nation can agree on a color symbolic of their patriotism, solidarity, and of course their expressed love. On the other hand, God created all living things, including people with a distinct and unique shade of *skin color* specific to their nation, and geographic location according to his divine appointment. *Skin Color,* "is the natural shade; or pigmentation of the skin." *Skin* is the largest organ that covers, protects, provides, and maintains all forms of life. For that reason, God created people with a distinctive color of skin to prosper on the earth according to where people live. In fact, every living thing, i.e. birds, fish, animals, insects, and plants are created with skin. As a matter of fact, no living thing exists without skin. Furthermore, nothing can change the color of its skin. Nonetheless, most people still reject the one true color of love symbolic of God's love − *skin color.* "Can you ever change and do what's right? Can people change the color of their skin, or can a leopard remove its spots? If so, then maybe you can change and learn to do right" (JEREMIAH 13:23 CEV).

Historically, flags are symbolic of an organization, state, or nation honoring its cultural diversity or to celebrate its isolationism. Generally speaking, a flag is "a piece of cloth, varying in size, shape, color, and design, usually attached to a staff or a cord." Realistically, a flag is more than symbolic because it serves to indicate the power, the strength, the determination, and the hope of a people united in solidarity by the colors, insignia, and design of their flag. Just as the flag of an organization, state, or nation warns any opponent of their independence.

With that in mind, the "Rainbow" flag serves to indicate the power, the strength, and the determination of the people that choose to live the LGBT (Lesbian, Gay, Bisexual, and Transgender) lifestyle. Currently, that 'Rainbow' flag is the most recognized symbol of LGBT solidarity.

Equally, the Nazi 'Swastika' (the motif a hooked cross) is symbolic of "Aryan purity" expressing the insane ideology of a racially "pure" world of people. For that reason, the Nazi 'Swastika' is one of the most recognized symbols of racial prejudice, racial intolerance, racial bigotry, and anti-Semitism expressed by fanatical people who fantasize about a make-believe world of racial purity. In the same way, the 'Rainbow' flag is symbolic of sexual bias, sexual bigotry, and sexual self-determination expressed by lascivious people who fantasize about a make-believe world dominated by homosexuals and bisexuals. Suffice to say, all rational thinking people utterly dismiss both of these insane fantasies, because clinically neither of these altered realities are sustainable.

On the subject of the lifestyle advocated within the LBGT community, their own definition of sexual classification is a choice, not a function necessary to live. Genetically, all living things were created with the distinction male and female. Scientifically, all living things were created with two basic elements needed to reproduce life the male sperm and the female egg. Factually, conception, pregnancy, and the birth of any living thing are impossible outside the reproductive design of God. In fact, doctors, scientists, and researchers can only confirm pregnancy, but they cannot know the moment conception occurs.

Nevertheless, people living the LBGT lifestyle utterly reject Gods reproductive design by categorically arguing that God "tripped up" when he assigned them their gender classifications.

For that reason, the LGBT communities' rationale for their sexual freedom, sexual self-determination, and changing their gender classification is this; "God made a grave error because he placed my soul in the wrong body." In fact, homosexuals say "biologically I am a boy, but in reality, I am a girl trapped in a boy's body." Likewise, "biologically I am a girl, but in reality, I am a boy trapped in a girl's body." Similarly, many people claim the moon is made of cheese, but that doesn't make it so. "You can rationalize it all you want and justify the path of error you have chosen, but you'll find out in the end that you took the road to destruction" (PROVERBS 14:12 TPT).

Biologically, God continues to prove he is the Creator of

all life by revealing the biochemistry sequencing of all life, i.e. DNA. *DNA* is, "deoxyribonucleic acid, a self-replicating material which is present in nearly all living organisms as the main constituent of chromosomes. *Chromosomes* are "any of several bodies, consisting of chromatin, that carries the genes in a linear order: the human species has 23 pairs, designated 1 to 22 in order of decreasing size and X and Y for the female and male chromosome respectively." Furthermore, DNA "reveals the fundamental and distinctive characteristics or qualities of someone or something, especially when regarded as unchangeable." Consequently, the unmerited allegation that God "tripped up" when he created both male and female distinctively is utterly baseless, because God created all living things with unchangeable qualities according to his reproductive design.

In fact, children instinctively know, recognize, and understand that it requires a male and a female to procreate. Likewise, children of all ages can clearly see how procreation is achieved watching nature. Nevertheless, people living the LBGT lifestyle purposely lie about that truth in an effort to groom children to engage in the most abominable sexual acts in rebellion to Gods reproductive design, arguing their sexual perversion is the truth, and that Gods reproductive design is a lie. Remember, homosexuals and bisexuals unanimously agree their sexual classification is a "life choice" because they are free to choose their own sexual preferences and their individual genders. "And so, since they did not see fit to acknowledge God *or* approve of Him *or* consider Him worth the knowing, God gave them over to a base *and* condemned mind to do things not proper *or* decent *but* loathsome. Though they are fully aware of God's righteous decree that those who do such things deserve to die, they not only do them themselves but approve *and* applaud others who practice them" (ROMANS 1:28, 32 AMP). Keep in mind; fleshly cut flowers are dead the moment they are separated (cut away) from the life-giving sap provided by the stem. Likewise, people that sever themselves from God are as flowers cut from the stem. Consequently, far too many people who practice the LGBT lifestyle die needlessly placing false confidence in their rebellious sexual behavior.

On the subject of Nazi separatist, white supremacist, and the murderous anti-Semitist that seek to create a racially "pure" nation of people. Similarly, their reasoning is so vile it's almost impossible to suppose. Suffice to say, all clear-thinking people agree that "no man" created all the living inhabitants of the earth. Just as all rational thinking people know, recognize, understand, and comprehend that no individual, no group, and no government have the authority to commit genocide, especially people of a particular ethnic group or nation in an attempt to create a man-made Utopian world. *Utopian* is "founded upon or involving idealized perfection; given to impractical or unrealistic schemes of such perfection." Likewise, these evil-minded people, i.e. Nazi separatist, white supremacist, white nationalist, and anti-Semitist also believe that God "tripped up" when he created people with the distinct and unchangeable *"color of love"— skin color.* Alternatively, their psychotic reality of a perfect "Aryan" race is a person of one *skin color* (pale), and one eye color (blue) that live under one narcissistic rule.

In the 1920s the Nazi party used anti-Semitism to create an animus against the Jewish population by claiming the Jewish people had an unfair economic advantage over the starving poor. In fact, most people during this era were economically poor, educationally ignorant, and had little hope their governments could recover from the atrocities of World War I. "The total number of military and civilian casualties in World War I was around 40 million. There were 20 million deaths and 21 million wounded. The total number of deaths includes 9.7 million military personnel and about 10 million civilians.[1]"

Still, during these brutal circumstances, the founders of the Nazi party seized on the opportunity to manipulate the thinking of millions of starving Germans by claiming the Jewish people were withholding the resources to keep them from starving. Cunningly, their purpose was to control the narrative so that a few narcissistic tyrants could seize total authoritarian control over the entire German population. Wickedly, in the aftermath of all this death, destruction, and suffering caused by World War I these megalomaniacs still believed a plan to create a "new world order" was achievable. Dreadfully, this quest for world supremacy dates back to the first egomaniac Cain the first son born of Adam and Eve.

Clinically speaking, Cain's psychosis was passed on through the DNA of his parents; Adam and Eve because of their severed relationship with God. However, God informed Cain beforehand, "Sin crouches at your door Cain, but I have given you the power to master it." *Sin* is "A thought, a word or a deed in direct violation of Gods righteous commands." Nevertheless, Cain's maniacal aspiration was world dominance. Consequently, he murdered his only brother Abel. Clearly, the murder of Abel by Cain was in direct violation of God's command, "Thou shall not kill." "For the wrath of God is revealed from heaven against all ungodliness and unrighteousness of men, who hold the truth in unrighteousness; Because that which may be known of God is manifest in them; for God hath shewed (showed) *it* unto them. For the invisible *things* that of him from the creation of the world are clearly seen, being understood by the things that are made, *even* His eternal power and Godhead; so that they are without excuse" (ROMANS 1:18-20 AMP). Nevertheless, white supremacist and the LBGT community still believe they are independent "free will" agents not answerable to God.

Similarly, white supremacist and the LGBT community share a common objective to proselytize (recruit, convert) as many feeble-minded people as possible to enthusiastically join in their narcissistic and lascivious behaviors. In fact, their combined strategy is to change the way people think over an extended period of time by mastering the use of Euphemisms.

Euphemisms are words "used as a mild substitute, indirect, or vague expression for one thought or known to be offensive, harsh, or blunt."

On the subject of the LGBT community, the word "homosexual" is a blunt word to define their abhorrent ungodly sexual behavior. Truthfully, no one will witness birds, fish, animals, or insects practicing such wanton sexual behavior. For that reason, the homosexual community realized they had to change the narrative by changing the public perception of their disgusting behavior. So, in the late 1970's the more palatable word "Gay" was chosen to replace the harsh term homosexuals. In the same way, homosexual women wanted their own sexual classification resulting in a new word "Lesbian."

Likewise, in the late 1990s, the LGBT community began using advanced medical technology to elevate their reckless behavior. At that moment medical science made it possible for homosexual men taking hormone therapy to alter their physiological appearance so that a man's breast could mimic the beast of women. As a result, the term "Transgender" became the official classification to replace the harsh term "drag queen" for men who feel they are a "woman" trapped in a man's body. In like manner, the LGBT community also replaced the harsh term bisexual with a new word "Queer.[2]"

Furthermore, the LBGT community also began an all-out public relations campaign falsely claiming heterosexuals were abusing them physically by the masses without any proof or any good reason. Still, the LBGT community made wild accusations, claiming they were victims of employment discrimination, housing discrimination, and medical discrimination, etc. In reality, most of their claims of discrimination were simply fabricated, because no one knew their sexual preferences until they parade it. Accordingly, to personify their purpose the LBGT community consistently used the psychological tactic, "He who shouts the loudest gets heard first" to validate their falsities. Truthfully, the only real discrimination claimed by the LGBT community is a result of their own sexual deviant behavior. Therefore, it's not what you say, or how loud you say it. Instead, "the only thing that counts is what you can prove."

To this end, God unequivocally proves that he is the Creator of all life because he explains every building block of life. Alternatively, the LBGT community and white supremacist cannot create life, sustain life or maintain any living thing including them. Realistically, their "pie in the sky" fantasies of a world dominated by sexual deviants and megalomaniacs only end in complete self-destruction and wholesale mass murder. This is what the LORD says: "Stop at the crossroads and look around. Ask for the old, godly way, and walk in it. Travel its path, and you will find rest for your souls. But you reply, 'No, that's not the road we want!' (Jeremiah 6:16 NLT)

CHAPTER 4

Color Me Beautiful

The greatest gift of all is life; God is the Creator of all life that's – truth. God created all people in his image and his likeness – that's proven. God's desire is that all people live in an unbroken relationship with him that's evident. God created all people to have children – that's unchangeable. Nevertheless, most people spend all of their lives ignoring God, denouncing God, or avoiding God all together – that's a fact. Without a doubt, most people hate the things of God because they attempt to destroy everything God created–that's real. On the other hand, people all over choose to worship the things God created, i.e. birds, fish, animals, and insects as their god – that's crazy. "But their idols are silver and gold, made by human hands. They have mouths, but cannot speak; they have ears, but cannot hear, noses, but cannot smell. They have hands, but cannot feel, feet, but cannot walk, nor can they utter a sound with their throats. Those who make them will be like them, and so will all who trust in them" (PSALM 155:4-8 NIV). Nonetheless, people all over continue to value the things God created greater than God.

So, why do people place a higher value on the things God created greater than God? Sorry to say most people don't appreciate the incalculable cost of human life. "But ask the animals, and they will teach you; the birds of the air, and they will tell you; ask the plants of the earth, and they will teach you; and the fish of the sea will declare to you. Who among all these does not know that the hand of the Lord has done this? In his hand is the life of every living thing and the breath of every human being" (JOB 12:7-10 NRS). On the other hand, people commit murder continuously without any justification, seek revenge without any reason, and purposely lie without any hesitation.

Historically, Cain was the first man who committed murder unjustifiably when he killed his brother Abel then denied any responsibility for his murderous act. Like Cain, most evil-minded people believe they are not answerable to God because they cannot see God. For that reason, people wrongly think they are free to commit murder without any punishment from God. Consequently, evil-minded people like Cain feel they have no restraint, no self-control, and no conscience. "And so, since they did not see fit to acknowledge God *or* approve of Him *or* consider Him worth the knowing, God gave them over to a base *and* condemned mind to do things not proper *or* decent *but* loathsome. Until they were filled (permeated and saturated) with every kind of unrighteousness, iniquity, grasping *and* malice. [They were] full of envy *and* jealousy, murder, strife, deceit *and* treachery, ill will *and* cruel ways. [They were] secret backbiters *and* gossipers. Slanderers, hateful to *and* hating God, full of insolence, arrogance, [and] boasting; inventors of new forms of evil, disobedient, *and* undutiful to parents. [They were] without understanding, conscienceless *and* faithless, heartless *and* loveless [and] merciless" (ROMANS 1:28-31 AMP). Actually, people all over the world live within these frightening conditions. Remember, *Fear* is a *living spirit* and opposes the things of God. Its intention is to vilify God, so people completely reject God as the source of human prosperity. In addition, the *spirit of fear* understands that people living in a continuous state of fear suffer from extreme anxiety. However, most people refuse to believe their decisions are being swayed by the *spirit of fear* because the *spirit of fear* is invisible. Instead, people believe "if they cannot see it then it's probably not real." On the other hand, everything known is not based on what people can taste, touch, smell, feel, or observe. In fact, all rational- minded people agree that you can feel the air, but you cannot see the air.

Nonetheless, the *spirit fear* uses that lack of knowledge to influence people to lie, to steal, to kill, and to destroy the things God created without any justification, without any reason, and without any hesitation. Orchestrating, all these evil acts in revenge because he did not get the one gift he prized above all gifts − Gods *skin color.*

Unequivocally, before the earth was formed Lucifer was the most beautiful angel in heaven. In spite of his unmatched beauty, Lucifer wanted to be a *"child"* of God made evident in the distinct and unique shades of *skin color.* So, Lucifer asked God to *"color me beautiful"* in your *skin color.* But, God denied Lucifer's request. At that moment, Lucifer became prideful and was cast out of heaven. "I appointed you to be like a guardian angel. I anointed you for that purpose. You were on my holy mountain. You walked among the gleaming jewels. Your conduct was without blame from the day you were created. But soon you began to sin. You traded with many nations. You harmed people everywhere. And you sinned. So I sent you away from my mountain in shame. Guardian angel, I drove you away from among the gleaming jewels. You thought you were so handsome that it made your heart proud. You thought you were so glorious that it spoiled your wisdom. So I threw you down to the earth. I made an example out of you in front of kings" (EZEZKIEL 28:14-17 NIRV). For that reason, Lucifer was stripped of his title and rank, and given the rebellious name – Satan; the *spirit of evil*; the *spirit of fear*; the *spirit of rebellion*; the *father of lies*; the *malicious accuser*; *the deceiver*; that old serpent [of primeval times], who is the *Devil*. Furthermore, God established the Garden of Eden to expose Satan, so that all creation could witness his sadistic acts.

In the Garden of Eden, Satan used Eve's lack of understanding as a weapon of psychological warfare when he questioned her about not eating of the fruit from the tree which is the middle of the garden. Clinically speaking, Satan used "reverse psychology" to cause Eve to want something else more desirable, specifically "to be wiser." *Reverse Psychology* is "A method of getting another person to do something by pretending not to want it or to want something else or someone else more."

"NOW THE serpent was more subtle *and* crafty than any living creature of the field which the Lord God had made. And he [Satan] said to the woman, Can it really be that God said, you shall not eat from every tree of this garden? And the woman said to the serpent, we may eat of the fruit from the trees of the garden. Except for the fruit from the tree which is in the middle of the garden. God has said you shall not eat of it; neither shall you touch it, lest you die. But the serpent said to the woman, you shall not surely die. For God knows that in the day you eat of it your eyes will be opened and you will be like God, knowing the difference between good and evil and blessings *and* calamity. And the woman saw that the tree was good (suitable, pleasant) for food and that it was delightful to look at, and a tree to be desired in order to make one wise, she took of its fruit and ate; and she gave some also to her husband" (GENESIS 3:1-6 AMP). At that moment, two cataclysmic events occurred simultaneously on the earth. First, Satan was exposed to all creation for plotting to deceive Eve. Simultaneously, Satan was titled the *"father of lies"* for tricking Eve into disobeying God.

Clearly, Satan understood he possessed the power to influence a picture that appeared vividly in Eve's mind using words. Keep in mind, Satan only questioned Eve to create a false image in her mind, "Can it really be that God has said; you shall not eat from every tree of this garden?" Remember, the true function of hearing is the ability to perceive a thing, or an event that appears vividly to the mind. Once more, God created people to see based on what they hear not based on what they see.

Deceitfully, Satan's aim was achieved when Eve imagined she would gain something more desirable by disobeying God's command, "And the woman saw that the tree was good for food, and that it was delightful to look at, and a tree to be desired in order to make one wise, so she took of its fruit and ate it." At that moment, Eve was cut away from God like a flower severed from the stem. Deviously, Satan planned all of these treacherous acts in revenge for being denied the one thing he desired above all things Gods — *skin color.*

Concurrently, when Adam ate the fruit it was also

an act of rebellion causing both Adam and Eve to suffer biologically in their bodies from the degrading effects sin. Instantly, their wicked nature passed through their DNA into the souls of every human being. Consequently, all people are born with a rebellious nature without any ability to change it. "And so people become enemies of God when they are controlled by their human nature; for they do not obey God's law, and in fact, they cannot obey it" (ROMANS 8:7 GNT). Therefore, people commit murder without any justification, seek revenge without any reason, and purposely lie without any hesitation, because it's in their "DNA."

CHAPTER 5

The Color of
Understanding

The color of love in a black and white world is written to provide the reader with the truthful answers to this multipart question people all over the world, pretend is unknowable, "Who created me and what is my purpose"? Simultaneously bringing an abrupt halt to the generational philosophical debates, endless theological arguments, and useless religious metaphors people at every point waste their time seeking to find an agreeable answer. Furthermore to provide the reader with a clear understanding of the origin of psychosis and why people cannot change their rebellious behavior. Specifically "Why people allow egomaniacs to commit mass murder without any penalty, governments to declare war without any justification, and people to purposely lie without any burden?" The truthful answer is this; most people believe they are not answerable to God.

"Shall the potter be considered of no more account than the clay? Shall the thing that is made say of its maker, He did not make me; or the thing that is formed say of him who formed it, He has no understanding?" (ISAIAH 29:16(b) AMPC). Nevertheless, most people are willing to spend a lifetime on a pointless quest to prove God isn't real. Consequently, people continue to repeat the same insane mistakes because apart from God people cannot change anything. "Those who cannot remember the past are condemned to repeat it." - George Santayana

Dreadfully, an estimated 20 million people were killed and an additional 21 million people wounded, and no one can accurately count the number of people who died from war-related injuries, displacement or other humanitarian crisis directly associated during World War I. Suffice to say the number of people killed and wounded is so vile it's almost impossible to suppose. All because of European nations fearing other neighboring nations would gain an economic, political, or military advantage. Consequently, European countries lived in a continuous state of anxiety, believing they would lose their independence. Living continuously under those frightful conditions the assassination of Archduke Franz Ferdinand is considered by historians as "the match that lit the fuse" starting War World I.

> World War I began in 1914 after the assassination of Archduke Franz Ferdinand and lasted until 1918. During the conflict, Germany, Austria-Hungary, Bulgaria and the Ottoman Empire (the Central Powers) fought against Great Britain, France, Russia, Italy, Romania, Japan, and the United States (the Allied Powers). Thanks to new military

technologies and the horrors of trench warfare, World War I saw unprecedented levels of carnage and destruction. By the time the war was over and the Allied Powers claimed victory, more than 16 million people—soldiers and civilians alike—were dead.[3]

After World War I, ended in 1918 people all over the world promised this mindless killing would never occur again. For that reason, the League of Nations was created in 1920 so countries could resolve their disputes diplomatically instead of going to war. The goal of the League of Nations was to craft a mutual agreement between nations to avoid mutual destruction between nations.

"The League of Nations was an international diplomatic group developed after World War I as a way to solve disputes between countries before they erupted into open warfare. A precursor to the United Nations, the League achieved some victories, but had a mixed record of success, sometimes putting self-interest before becoming involved in conflict resolution, while also contending with governments that did not recognize its authority. The League effectively ceased operations during World War II.[4]" Clearly, the combined wisdom of the 32 nations who signed the "Treaty of Versailles" June 28, 1919, did not prevent the same error of thinking because 21 years later in 1938, the world was at war again. "If you fail to plan, you are planning to fail." –Benjamin Franklin

Pathetically, people all over the world believe that "all they need to know is what they want to know" in order to achieve success or to avoid tragedy. Realistically, nothing could be further from the truth because historically people all over the world continue to prove they are incapable of avoiding the same catastrophic errors of judgment based on presumptuous information. Honesty, no one is capable of knowing when a thought or what thoughts will enter into their minds. Furthermore, people do not independently create or control the origins of their thoughts, however, people can decide whether to dismiss or entertain a though when it enters into their minds. In fact, God created all people with the ability to change their minds.

Clinically speaking people who cannot understand and do not recognize their delusional thinking suffer from a mental deficiency diagnosed as psychosis. *Psychosis* is "A mental disorder characterized by symptoms, such as delusions or hallucinations, that indicate impaired, contact with reality; any severe form of mental disorder, as schizophrenia or paranoia." In other words, people who expect to get a different result but cannot change the way they think about someone or something are considered psychotic (mentally unstable). With that in mind, in 1938 World War II broke out bringing an abrupt end to the League of Nations, proving the combined wisdom of the 32 member nations failed to prevent the maniacal leaders of European nations from repeating the same insane decisions. "There is a way that seems right to a man, but its end is the way to death" (PROVERBS 14:12 ESV). In fact, history is the absolute proof that people cannot change their murderous nature, their passive attitudes regarding the atrocities they witness, and their willingness to wholeheartedly accept a lie as the truth.

The instability created in Europe by the First War (1914-18) set the stage for another international conflict-World-War II-which broke out two decades later and would prove even more devastating. Rising to power in an economically and politically unstable Germany, Adolf Hitler and his National Socialist (Nazi Party) rearmed the nation and signed strategic treaties with Italy and Japan to further his ambitions of world domination. Hitler's invasion of Poland in September 1939 drove Great Britain and France to declare war on Germany, and World War II had begun. Over the next six years, the conflict would take more lives and destroy more land and property around the globe than any previous war. Among the estimated, 45-60 million people killed 6 million Jews were murdered in Nazi concentration camps as part of Hitler's diabolical "Final Solution", now known as the Holocaust.[5]

Wickedly, after all this death, carnage, and suffering people still placed their complete confidence in the wisdom of men, instead of getting an understanding from God. "Self-confident know-it-alls will prove to be fools. But when you lean on the wisdom from above, you will have a way to escape the troubles of your own making" (PROVERBS 28:26 TPT). Nonetheless, people all over the world would rather die ignorant than accept instruction from God.

Predictably at the end of World War II, another fool hearted plan was created by so-called wise leaders from all over the world in a futile attempt to police the world by establishing the United Nations. The United Nations goal was to prevent the atrocities of World War I from occurring again by finding "diplomatic solutions to end conflicts between nations" beforehand. In fact, the New York, New York-based UN offers this cleverly worded mission statement on the "home page" of its website;

> The United Nations is an international organization founded in 1945 after the Second World War by 51 countries committed to maintaining international peace and security, developing friendly relations among nations and promoting social progress, better living standards, and human rights. Due to its unique international character, and the powers vested in its founding Charter, the Organization can take action on a wide range of issues, and provide a forum for its 193 Member States to express their views, through the General Assembly, the Security Council, the Economic and Social Council and other bodies and committees. The work of the United Nations reaches every corner of the globe. Although best known for peacekeeping, peacebuilding, conflict prevention and, humanitarian assistance, there are many other ways the United Nations and its Systems (specialized agencies, funds, and programs) affect our lives and make the world a better place.[6]

Honestly, nothing in this mission statement is based on reality, because each member country is motivated by self-interest. In fact, the United Nations has no real power because the 193 member nations cannot unanimously agree

on anything—especially deploying peacekeeping troops
were mass murder and genocides occur continuously.

A report assessing the United Nations
involvement in Rwanda said on its release
Thursday that the UN and its member states
failed Rwanda in deplorable ways in 1994,
ignoring evidence that genocide was planned,
refusing to act once it was underway, and
finally abandoning the Rwandan people
when they most needed protection. The
independent report, commissioned by
Secretary-General Kofi Annan, showed
a UN peacekeeping mission in Rwanda
doomed from the start by an insufficient
mandate and later destroyed by the Security
Council's refusal to strengthen it once the
killings began. And it showed UN officials -
Annan and then-Secretary-General Boutros
Boutros-Ghali among them - unable or
unwilling to act on information from the
field that a massive slaughter was occurring
and that they needed to do something to
stop it. The United Nations launched its
peacekeeping mission for Rwanda in October
1993 to monitor a cease-fire agreement
between the Rwandan Hutu government and
the rebel Rwandese Patriotic Front.

The mission, that was not allowed to use
military force to achieve its aims, was limited
to investigating breaches in the cease-fire,
helping humanitarian aid deliveries, and
contributing to the security of the capital,

Kigali. The mission proved insufficient after the government launched the slaughter of an estimated 800,000 minority Tutsis and moderate Hutus following the downing of the Rwandan president's plane on April 6, 1994. The report faulted the United Nations in several key areas leading up to that date, including its failure to act on a now-famous cable sent by the force commander, Canadian Lt. Gen. Romeo Dallaire on Jan. 11, 1994 warning of the risk of genocide. The cable was received by Annan and wasn't shared with the Security Council and didn't receive the follow-up such an important piece of evidence deserved, the report said.

In addition, the United Nations and Security Council virtually ignored a groundbreaking assessment by the UN human rights investigator in Rwanda who raised the possibility in August 1993 that genocide might occur.[7]

Factually, between April 7, 1994, and July 1994 some NGO's (Non-government organizations) estimate that 1 million people were killed in Rwanda while the United Nations did nothing to intervene. That means that approximately 83,333.33 people were slaughtered needlessly every day for 120 consecutive days. Needless to say, the United Nations is incapable of negotiating a diplomatic solution before genocides occur; deploy adequate resources when a humanitarian crisis occurs, moreover, the willpower to eliminate the economic, political, and military conditions that start wars. Consequently, the United Nations is a useless international organization in solving any local, national, or international crisis because the United Nations is incapable of reaching a unanimous consensus. "It does a fool no good to spend money on an education, because he has no common sense" (PROVERBS 17:16 GNT).

Equally sinister and just as deadly are the estimated 79 million premeditated deaths caused by the sexual behavior of the LBGT community. Specifically, the outbreak of the worst epidemic in the modern era –HIV/AIDS. Despite being fully aware of God's righteous decree that those who practice, applaud, or passively condone the LBGT lifestyles deserve to die because of the atrocities resulting from their backward sexual behavior. Deliberately, people living the LBGT lifestyle completely reject God righteous decree that no living thing does such debased sexual acts. Furthermore, people living the LBGT lifestyle mock God by flaunting and parading their vile behavior in the sight of God daring him to punish them. "Do not be deceived *and* deluded *and* mislead; God will not allow Himself to be sneered at (scorned, disdained, or mocked by mere pretensions or professions, or by His precepts being set aside.) [He inevitably deludes himself, who attempts to delude God.] For whatever a man sows, that *and* that only is what he will reap" (GALATIANS 6:7 AMPC).

Wickedly, people living LBGT lifestyle craftily hide the truth about the deadly consequences of their sexually deviant behavior from naive people all over the world, especially children they specifically target to recruit. Remember, the combined goal of the LGBT community is to live in a world dominated by homosexuals and bisexuals. Perversely, their strategy is to parade their backward sexual lifestyle so obviously it will be accepted as normal. Ultimately their aim is to prove their psychotic *sexual-truth* that God "made a grave error" because he assigned their gender classifications without permission. "You shall know the truth, and the truth shall set you free" (JOHN 8:32 MEV). Truthfully, nothing about the "Gay" lifestyle is attractive.

The history of HIV is filled with triumphs and failures as the world faced what would become the greatest global epidemic of modern times. What began with but a handful of infections grew to a pandemic that today affects over 36 million people worldwide. The HIV timeline began early in 1981 when the New York Times reported an outbreak of a rare form of cancer among gay men in New York and California. This "gay cancer" as it was later identified as Kaposi sarcoma, a disease that later became the very face of the disease in the 1980s and 1990s. In that same year, emergency rooms in New York City began to see a rash of otherwise healthy young men presenting with fevers, flu-like symptoms, and a rare type of pneumonia called *Pneumocystis*. No one could have imagined that these unusual, isolated cases would foreshadow a global outbreak, killing millions of people within the course of a few years.

1981- The emergence of Kaposi sarcoma and Pneumocystis pneumonia among gay men in New York and California. When the Centers for Disease Control reported the new outbreak, they christened it GRID (or gay-related immune deficiency), stigmatizing the gay community as carriers of the deadly disease. However, cases soon started to appear among heterosexuals, drug users, and hemophiliacs, proving the syndrome knew no boundaries.

1983 - Researchers at the Pasteur Institute in France isolated a retrovirus that they believe is related to the outbreak of HIV. By that time, 35 countries around the world had confirmed cases of the disease that had, up until that point, only appeared to affect the U.S. Controversy arose soon after when the U.S. government announced one of their scientists, Dr. Robert Gallo, had isolated a retrovirus called HTLV-III, which they claimed was responsible for AIDS. Two years later, it is finally confirmed that HTLV-III and the Pasteur retroviruses are the same, leading an international committee to rename the virus HIV (human immunodeficiency virus).

1984 - A Canadian flight attendant, dubbed "Patient Zero," dies of AIDS-related complications. Because of his sexual connection to several of the first victims of HIV, it is erroneously reported that he is responsible for introducing the virus into North America. By this time there were 8,000 confirmed cases in the U.S., resulting in 3,500 deaths.

1985 -The controversy surrounding HIV continues when Gallo's lab patents an HIV test kit that later is approved by the U.S. Food and Drug Administration (FDA). The Pasteur Institute sues and is later awarded rights to half of the royalties from the new test. In that same year, HIV enters the public consciousness with the death of Rock Hudson and news that 14-year-old Ryan White is barred from his elementary school in Indiana for having HIV.

1992 - The FDA approves the first drug to be used in combination with AZT known as Hivid, marking the medical community's first foray into combination therapy. It is followed soon after by Epivir (lamivudine) which is still commonly used today.

1993 - A British study known as the Concorde Trials concludes that AZT immunotherapy does nothing to delay progression to HIV. As a result of this report, a new movement emerges to deny that HIV exists or that a virus of any sort is even linked to the disease.

1996 - Treatment takes another major step forward with the introduction of power HIV drugs called Protease Inhibitors. When used in triple therapy, the drugs prove effective in not only suppressing the virus but enabling people to restore the immune system to near-normal levels. The protocol is immediately dubbed highly active antiretroviral therapy or HAART.

1997 - The AIDS Clinical Trials Group study 076 reported that the use of AZT during pregnancy and at the time of delivery reduced the transmission of HIV from mother to child to just three percent. In that same year, less than 12 months after HAART is introduced, the HIV death rate in the U.S. plummets by 35 percent.

1998 -The first human trials in the United States begin to test the VAXGEN HIV vaccine. (It was the first of many such trials for which we have yet to find a viable candidate.)

2000 -The AIDS denialist movement gets international attention when South African president Thabo Mbeki declares at the International AIDS Conference that "a virus cannot cause a syndrome." By this time, nearly 20 million people have died from AIDS worldwide including nearly 17 million in sub-Saharan Africa.

2004 - As the medical community is faced with a growing tide of drug resistance among people on HAART, a new drug called tenofovir is released which appears able to overcome even cases of deep, multi-drug resistance. Shortly before Thabo Mbeki is ejected from the presidency in South Africa, the first generic HIV drugs are approved in the country, opening the door to the single-largest drug treatment roll-out in history.

2009 - Scientists at the University of North Carolina at Chapel Hill announce they have decoded the structure of an entire HIV genome, allowing scientist to develop newer diagnostic tools and targeted treatment for HIV. It is largely this effort that led to the development of integrase inhibitors which are now used for the first-line treatment in the U.S

2010 - The iPrEX study is the first of many trials which shows that the HIV drug Truvada could be used by HIV-negative people to prevent getting infected. The strategy, known as HIV pre-exposure prophylaxis (PrEP), is today commonly prescribed to protect people at high risk of infection.

2013 - A study conducted by North American AIDS Cohort Collaboration on Research and Design (NA-ACCORD) reports that a 20-year-old started on HIV therapy can expect to live well into his or her early 70s. This is the first of many such confirmations describing the impact of antiretroviral therapy on life expectancy.

2014 - The World Health Organization and the United Nations Program on HIV/AID (UNAIDS) announces an ambitious plan to end the HIV pandemic by 2030 by diagnosing 90 percent of people living with HIV worldwide, placing 90 percent on HIV therapy, and achieving an undetectable viral load in 90 percent of those. Dubbed the 90-90-90 strategy, the program is faced with ever-shrinking contributions from donor countries and ever-increasing rates of drug resistance and treatment failures worldwide.

2015 -Indiana experiences the largest outbreak of HIV since the 1990s due to widespread opioid epidemic and resistance by then-Governor Mike Pence to allow a needle exchange program in his state on "moral grounds." As a result, over 200 cases are reported within a few weeks in and around the town of Austin, Indiana (population 4,295).

2016 - Following the release of the Strategic Timing of Antiretroviral Treatment (START) study in late-2015, the World Health Organization and the U.S. Department of Health and Human Service, among others, recommends that HIV treatment be started at the time of diagnosis. As opposed to delaying treatment, the new strategy has been proven to reduce the risk of serious illness by 53 percent.

2017 - Now in its 36th year, the epidemic continues to claim a million lives each year and adds another 1.8 million new infections to the tally in 2017. There are now an estimated 36.7 million people living with

HIV worldwide of which 20.9 million are on antiretroviral therapy. In total, over 76 million people have been infected with HIV since the start of the pandemic of which 35 million people have died.[8]

Finally, God has repeatedly proven that he will not allow human ingenuity, i.e. scientific or medical research to supersede his word. "So shall my word be that goeth forth out of my mouth: it shall not return unto me void, but it shall accomplish that which I please, and it shall prosper in the thing whereto I sent it" (ISAIAH 55:11 KJV). Therefore, people living the LBGT lifestyle die needlessly placing false confidence in their rebellious sexual behavior. Remember, the LBGT definition of sexual classification is a "life choice", not a function necessary to live.

BIBLE TRANSLATIONS

(AMP)   AMPLIFIED

(AMCP)   AMPLIFIED CLASSIC EDITION

(CEV)   COMTEMPOARY ENGLISH VERSION

(CSB)   CHRISTIAN STANDARD

(ERV)   EASY TO READ VERSION

(ESV)   ENGISH STANDARD VERSION

(GNT)   GOOD NEWS TRANSLATION

(GW)   GODS WORD TRANSLATION

(ISV)   INTERNATIONAL STANDARD VERSION

(KJV)   KING JAMES VERSION

(NASB)   NEW AMERICAN STANDARD BIBLE

(NIV)   NEW INTERNATIONAL VERSION

(NIRV)   NEW INTERNATIONAL REVISED VERSION

(NLT)   NEW LIVING TRANSLATION

(NRS)   NEW REVISED STANDARD

(TPT)   THE PASSION TRANSLATION

BIBLIOGRAPHY

[1] REPERES—module 1-0 – explanatory notes—World War 1 casualties – EN Author & ©: Nadege Mougel, CVCE, 2011 www.census.gov/history/pdf/reperes112018.pdf

[2] LBGT(or GLBT) initialism, Replacing the word "Gay" https://en.wikipcdia.org/wiki/LGBT

[3] World War 1, HISTORY.COM EDITORS, OCT 29, 2009 www.history.com/topics/world-war-i/world-war-i-history

[4] League of Nations, HISTORY.COM EDITORS, OCT 12, 2017 www.history.com/topics/world-war-i/league-of-nations

[5] World War II, HISTORY.COM EDITORS, OCT 29, 2009 www.history.com/topics/world-war-ii/world-war-ii-history#section_3

[6] History of the UN, United Nations © 2015. New York, NY 10017 www.un.org/un70/en/content/history/index.html

[7] Nicole Winfield, "UN Failed Rwanda", Associated Press / *Nando Media*, December 16, 1999 www.globalpolicy.org/component/content/article/201-rwanda/39240.html

[8] Mark Cichocki, RN, A brief History of HIV, 'Key Moments in the Fight Against the greatest Global Epidemic', VERYWELLheatlth, updated August 21, 2019 https://www.verywellhealth.com/the-history-of-hiv-49350

Printed in the United States
By Bookmasters